Dedicated To
All Software Professionals

|| Thank you All ||

"The World is full of magical things waiting for our wits to
grow sharper"
EDEN PHILLPOTTS (1862-1960)

"Miracles are not contrary to nature but only contrary to
what we know
about nature"
CATHOLIC BISHOP

Contents

Forwards

It was in 1995 in the month of August when college exams were over, and I wanted to learn something, well to be honest I did not know exactly what that something was. And it was true for all my hostel mates too. After a week was passed and then I had a quest to learn computers, well that's what it was called then. It was later I came to know that it's not "Learn Computers" but its learning computers languages and how to use computers.

So, the journey was started back then and after completing many milestones I was part of IT industry and was working as an IT professional with one the best software companies in Mumbai.

Before I could get this high paying job, a lot was put into action. I started off as a dBase III+ programmer in 1997, that was the year I was out of college completing my graduation. Then I learned FoxPro and worked as an instructor in 1998. At that time there were very few opportunities and finding a good job was harder than today is.

After working for couple years, I thought of upgrading my skills and then went on to join a full-time course in Mumbai which had been instrumental in shaping my career as it is today. When that course was about to complete, I got placement opportunities in some of the best IT companies like Syntel, Asian Paint. But I had something else in my mind so decided to join a far smaller company which was working on latest technologies.

That was where I honed my IT skills and then after working there for few years I never looked back. I have commanded highest salary in the industry though out and until today.

Now I work as a Software Architect in on the fast-growing American company.

So why I was talking about all this. Well I wanted to through some light on the things that were my friends and guides throughout this marvellous journey

Any guess? well here it is the "BOOKS" or rather "Computer Books".

Every weekend I used to go computer book shops and try to find some good book on computers, those days these eBooks were not there, so finding a good book shop was also one tasks. But then it was so much interesting work that one could enjoy it. I always enjoyed that.

I am thankful to all the books that I read, and I will remain thankful to those books forever.

So that's one the reason I am writing this book, I want to provide a good learning book which can help IT professional to enhance their skill. And I will be delighted if that happens, I am confident though.

At the end this book I have a section for feedback, so use that, once you are done reading this book.

Thank you for reading this far. And I wish Very Happy Learning

|| ALL THE BEST ||

Acknowledgements

There are so many people whom I want to be thankful to. My heart goes to my father Soran Singh who took this responsibility of shaping my life in the best possible manner he could, well it was like everybody else's father though, but sometimes I think he went few extra miles than anybody else. And those were the things that mattered a lot and because of that only today I am able to put these words together here. Thank you, dearest father, for making me this able.

Then it's my family, my wife Eakta who did lots of typing and kids Neel and Vishnu who let my wife work on this book even though they needed her. I should not forget my mother who always keeps on inspiring me by her small rustic quotes.

And want to thank Amazon for publishing this book.

And at last I want to thank each, and everyone involved in making this book happen.

Thank you Thank you Thank you!!!

Introduction

Let's talk about what this book is all about.

Well the idea behind writing this book on ASP. Net Web API is simple. I wanted to have a learning material to be available in market which can help people in enhancing their skill in ASP. Net Web API Restful service development in the fastest possible way.

ASP.net web API is gaining momentum and still going on. There is a possibility of a new technology coming in and taking over ASP. Net Web API, but as of today the Web API restful services are in swing.

The reason why this technology is so popular is that we can create ASP.Net Web API service which can be used by any client whatsoever.

How much time to read this book

7 days or Less than that may be 1 or 2.

The book can be easily covered in 7 days. Some will finish it early and some may take little longer based on individual pace.

There are 7 Chapters in this book

1st Covers basics

2nd Covers API Development and its usage.

3rd Covers Routing features

4th Covers API Data formats

5th Covers Unit Testing

6th Covers Deployment and API hosting.

7th Cover Advance Topics

8th Cover the Learning Evaluation.

Feedback

And at the end there is section for learners' feedback – please send your feedback. So that we can improve this book.

Before we begin Quiz

I have created a set of 10 questions which I want you to go through before started off reading the book, this will help you in understanding how much you Already know about ASP. Net Web API

Q1. ASP.NET Web API is a framework that simplifies building HTTP services for broader range of clients (including browsers as well as mobile devices) on top of .NET Framework. Using ASP.NET Web API we can create non-SOAP based services like plain XML or JSON strings etc.

a) True b) False

Q2. ASP. Net Web API works the way HTTP do using standard HTTP verbs like GET, POST, PUT, DELETE etc for all CRUD operations.

a) True b) False

Q3 Is it true that ASP.NET Web API has replaced WCF?

a) True b) False

Q4 ASP.NET WEB API is soap based like WCF

a) True b) False

Q5 How to return View from ASP.NET Web API method?

a) Using Action Result as return type in Api Controller
b) By returning an Mvc partial view
c) No, we cannot return view from web api method

Q6 How to restrict access to Web API method to specific HTTP Verb

a) By adding config section mappings
b) By enabling attribute routing in Web API
c) By applying an [httppost] attribute to method.

Q7 Can we use Web API with ASP.NET Web Form

a) True b) False

Q8 How we can provide an alias name for ASP.NET Web API action?

a) Enabling attribute routing in API Config.
b) By using Action attribute and enabling attribute routing in API Config
c) By using a custom MediaType formatter

Q9 ASP.NET Web API creates simple HTTP services that renders raw data.

a) True b) False

Q10 More new features introduced in ASP.NET Web API framework v2.0 are as follows.

a) Attribute Routing.
b) CORS.
c) IHttpActionResult.
d) OWIN self-hosting.
e) All of the above

Note down your score and compare it with final evaluation score at the end.

ASP. Net Web API - Introduction

What is Web API?

ASP dot net Web API is a framework that makes it easy to build HTTP services that reach a broad range of clients, including browsers and mobile devices.

ASP dot net Web API is an ideal platform for building Restful applications on the .NET Framework.

HTTP & Web API

HTTP protocol is not just for serving up web pages. It is also a powerful platform for building APIs that expose services and data. HTTP is simple, flexible.

Almost any platform that you can think of has an HTTP library, so HTTP services can reach a broad range of clients, including browsers, mobile devices, and traditional desktop applications.

Here is the list of topics which are part of this book.

1. Starting with ASP.Net Web API
2. Using ASP.Net Web API with Microsoft Entity Framework

3. Supporting OData Query Options in ASP.Net Web API
4. Doing CRUD with ASP.Net Web API
5. Routing in ASP.Net Web API
6. Attribute Routing in ASP.Net Web API
7. ASP.Net Web API and Exception Handling
8. Media Formatters in ASP.Net Web API
9. JSON and XML Serialization in ASP.Net Web API
10. BSON Support in ASP.Net Web API 2.1
11. Unit Testing Controllers in ASP.Net Web API
12. OWIN to Self-Host ASP.Net Web API
13. Hosting Web Api in Cloud with Azure
14. Hosting ASP.Net Web API in IIS & IIS Express
15. Using Https with ASP.Net Web API
16. Unit Testing and mocking with Entity Framework in Asp.Net Web API
17. Authenticating and Authorization in Asp.Net Web API

Who should read this book?

The book is designed for .NET Developers, Tech Leads and Architects who are working on Microsoft technologies like ASP dot net, ASP dot net MVC for developing web and mobile based applications.

What will you be learning?

After completion the learner will be able to develop ASP dot net Web API services comfortably.

What are the requirements?

1. Some background in .NET development

2. Knows how to use visual studio
3. Good to have: Experience ASP.Net MVC

What am I going to get from this book?

1. To develop competence in developing ASP. Net Web API with C#
2. Understanding ASP. Net web API fundamentals
3. Acquire skills required for api developer

Who are the target readers?

1. Freshers who want to get into IT industry
2. .NET Developers who want to enhance their skills
3. IT Professionals

Chapter - 1
Starting with ASP .Net Web API

ASP.Net

ASP.NET is Microsoft's free web framework which can used for building web applications using HTML, CSS, jQuery, C# and JavaScript. The framework can also be used for creating **Web APIs.**

ASP.Net now have featured technologies like SignalR and Web Sockets which can used for creating real-time application behaviour.

ASP.NET and web applications

We can use ASP.NET frameworks for creating web applications in the following ways

1. Creating Web Forms based applications

2. Creating ASP.NET MVC Applications

3. Creating ASP.NET Web Pages.

ASP.NET have separate framework for each of the approach mentioned. And these frameworks have been used across Industries for developing and maintaining web application. All three frameworks have become very stable and mature.

You can use any of the frameworks for developing web application, All ASP.NET features and will be there for you to get the benefit of.

Each of the above-mentioned frameworks are having its own style of development.

So, with ASP.NET you get options of choosing one of the frameworks which suits your

1. Skills

2. Development Experience

3. Knowledge of technology

4. Application Type

5. Development approach

You find the detailed overview of each of the framework. Also, there will be tips on which framework is more suitable for which business need and why.

Framework You Choose	Least Skill Required	Development approach you are looking for	Level of expertise in your team
Web Forms	Win Forms, WPF, .NET	RAD With rich out of the box controls for HTML mark-up	Mid, Advanced RAD
MVC	Ruby on Rails, .NET	SPA, Easy Unit Testing, Mobile based apps	Mid, Advanced

		Code and HTML in same file	Mid-Level, Fresher
Web Pages	PHP, Classic ASP		

Web Forms

Using ASP.NET Web Forms based framework of ASP.NET, We have choice of building dynamic websites using HTML control drag-and-drop and event-driven model.

ASP.Net Web forms framework comes with a rich library of hundreds of controls and components that can utilized for developing web application in very rapid manner. With help of this framework we can build rich UI web apps having database access capabilities.

MVC

ASP.NET MVC framework provides developers the following features

1. Patterns-based approach for building dynamic web apps

2. Having clear separation of concerns

3. Full control over mark-up

4. ASP.NET MVC has got many features which help in Rapid Application Development

5. TDD based development

6. Usage of current and trending web standards.

Web Pages - ASP.NET

ASP.NET Web Pages based framework provides the following features to the developer

1. Razor syntax. With Razor syntax you can create application having server-side code and HTML mark-up together in single file which makes it possible to generate dynamic content which can database driven.

2. Databases connectivity,

3. Capability of adding videos on the web pages,

4. Capability of linking social networking site profile,

5. And Many more features

More on these three frameworks

Web Pages, Web Forms and MVC

Microsoft .Net framework is at the root of all these frameworks of ASP.NET frameworks so all these frameworks have the core features and functionality of .NET and of ASP.NET.

Here are few examples

1. Same security model, ASP.Net membership-based login feature

2. Same web request management features

3. Same sessions management

Note: All these three frameworks are not exclusive to each other, mean if you are using one of them it does not mean the other two cannot used. Since core .Net framework is sitting at the bottom which includes all three.

A developer can easily utilize more than one framework in the same application.

For example, you can develop web facing sections of a web application in MVC and the intranet based or the inhouse usage sections of the same application can be developed using web forms.

ASP.NET Web APIs

Microsoft came up with a framework for developing http-based service and this framework is based on ASP.NET MVC. and they called it ASP.NET Web API framework.

With the help of ASP.Net Web Api framework we can create simple http or https-based services which in the background are quite similar to MVC web Apps.

These services do not expose an interface like WCF does. Rather they have an api controller where web api methods are defined. These methods are also called api action methods like MVC.

So how Web API framework expose these methods to the clients?

Web Api framework have something called api routing, with this feature a web api defines the client callable URI and these URI are mapped back to the corresponding api action methods by something called Routing table.

In this chapter we are going to discuss the following topics further.

1. Why Web API.
2. What Problems doe it solves for us.
3. Best API usages
4. Creating a simple web API

Why Web API?

Well we all know that it's the time IOT and there are so many devices which are out there, which are used by people in their day to day life. Now all these devices function with internet and use apps and data from various data stores/sources.

To get data to the apps running on these devices we need some kind service which a device can call and get the required stuff from it.

For this purpose, ASP. Net API seems to be or rather is a good fit. Because the Web Api is http based and can be consumed by any device which can interact with internet.

What problem does ASP. Net API solves?

Before ASP. Net Web API we have WCF which we could use to create Restful services. But if you remember and had developed a WCF restful service then you might know that it requires tweaking in order to make it consumable by various devices.

Also, WCF is soap based but web API is not.

Best API usages

ASP. Net Web API Services can be used in places where there is a requirement of using the same service for data vending to various types of application like web application, Windows Phone, iPhone, tablets etc.

Creating Your First Web API Service.

For creating an ASP. Net Web API service we need Microsoft Visual Studio. Its good if you guys have latest version of Visual Studio. If you have some hand on knowledge of Visual Studio then it's great, otherwise it's a very easy to use IDE. You can learn it very quickly.

So here are the steps that we need to perform to create an ASP. Net Web API in MS Visual Studio.

1. Open Visual Studio in Admin mode, for that you can right click on visual studio icon on your pc and select "Run as Administrator" as shown below

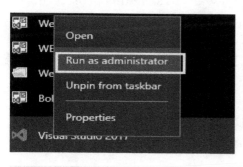

Once the visual studio is open the next step is

2. Go to **File** menu
3. Select **New** then select **Project**

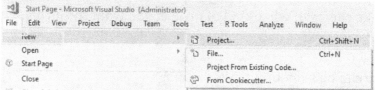

When you click on **Project,** a window pane will open then

4. Select "Web" in left pane and then select "Asp.Net Web Application" **Project Template** from the **Template** list in the pane as shown below.

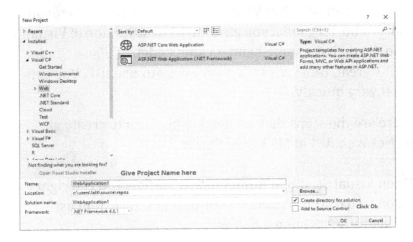

As you can here you can give your **project a name** and then select the **location** where you want to save this project file on your computer hard disk.

Then choose the target **.NET Framework version** and then click "**OK**"

when you click "OK" Visual Studio will open another window pane for you, where you need to select

or make choice of what kind of project you want this project to be.

Choice can be something like

Blank project, MVC, API etc

As shown below

Here in this windows pane you can see that we can select 6 different kind of **Project Templates**.

Since here we are creating a Web API service, so we will select
Web API Project Template and click **OK**

When we click **OK**, Visual Studio will create **a Web API Project** for us.

Now if you are latest version of visual studio then it will do nuget for all the dependencies of the API project

So initially it will take some time to create it and also to build and run it.

When you see the project structure in visual studio solution explorer you will notice that there are quite a lot of file and folders.

So out of these file and folder there few which are important to look at.

App_Start folder, this folder contains API configuration files. And that project in Solution Explorer will look something like this

As you can see here there are four file which **Web API application** use for managing its configuration. Now out of these four, one of them is very important to understand that is "**WebApiConfig.cs**" this is where web api define the following things.

1. Base API Route
2. Enable Attribute Routing
3. Enable a custom MediaFormater
4. Apply Exception Filters
5. Enable OData Query support

The other config classes are used for various other settings like specific **routing, bundling, and applying filters**.

Then we have API controller's folder where web API controllers are kept.

```
▲  🗀 Controllers
    ▷   C# EmployeeController.cs
    ▷   C# HomeController.cs
    ▷   C# ProductsController.cs
▷  🖿 fonts
    🖿 Models
▷  🖿 Scripts
▷  🖿 Views
▷  🗋 ApplicationInsights.config
    🖹 favicon.ico
▷  🗋 Global.asax
```

And one more thing to note here is this Global.asax file where application start up events are placed, when a web api application is loaded first time these events get fired and the code or setting which we keep in these events will run at that time.

In ASP.Net Web API, a controller is a class which handles HTTP incoming requests. It defines all the api action methods.

If you are familiar with ASP.NET MVC, then you must be knowing what a controller is.

In Web API also, we have controllers which are like to MVC controllers only

With One difference and that api controllers inherit the Api Controller class while MVC controllers inherit the Controller class.

Now let's have a look at **API controller class,** it looks something like this

```
public class ProductsController : ApiController
{
    IEmployeeBL iEmployeeBL = new EmployeeBL();

    public Product Get(){...}

    public void Post([FromBody]string value){...}

    public void Put(int id, [FromBody]string value){...}

    public void Delete(int id){...}
}
```

As you can see here it has all the API method signatures by default like **Get, Post, Put and Delete**

We can use these api methods and override these methods with different signatures.

Now since we have created a web api project in visual studio and have discussed the most important components in this project.

Let's try to run this API application and see what happens.

To run this api in this case we also have a web application where our **API controllers** are kept together. We can separate api controllers from the web App if want to.

Visual Studio by default creates this web app for us, which we can use to get **web API related help and test the api** .

I will show you that when we will run the api application.

To run the App just click on the **RUN** button in visual studio where **Web Server** name and **browser** names are given. It looks like this.

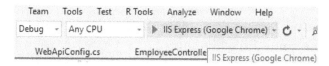

So when you click on this button, visual studio will build the **solution and projects** in it.

And then it will start the **web server**, which is **IIS Express** in this case and then launch the app in the selected **browser** which is Chrome in this case

Once the app is running then we can initiate the calls to **API Controller Methods,** Before we can do that lets understand the Api Routing

In this case if you take a look at the **WebApiConfig.cs** file, it defines a **default Route** for the **API calls** and it looks something like this

```
config.Routes.MapHttpRoute(
    name: "DefaultApi",
    routeTemplate: "Api/{controller}/{id}",
    defaults: new { id = RouteParameter.Optional }
);
```

The way Api URI is defined here is "/api/controllername/id"

Now if I want to call Get method for this Api on **ProductsController,** I will have to use the following URI.

http://localhost:portnumber/api/Products

when we run and use this URI in browser, Get method on Products controller will be called and data will be returned to the browser.

The results will be something like this.

```
This XML file does not appear to have any style information associated with it. The document tree is shown below.

▼<Product xmlns:i="http://www.w3.org/2001/XMLSchema-instance" xmlns="http://schemas.datacontract.org/2004/07/EmployeeVM">
    <price>100</price>
    <productid>1</productid>
    <productname>Product1</productname>
  </Product>
```

Chapter Recap

So in this chapter we discussed about the basic concept of ASP. Net Web API.

And created a very basic web api service and tried to run that in and see the results of
Get Method.

Chapter - 2

CRUD Operations with Web Api using Entity Framework

Web API with Entity Framework

In this chapter we are going to use entity framework 6 to get data from SQL Server Database. For that we will see what are the things that need to be done.

We will use **Database First** approach here for Entity Framework 6

And the we will create an **edmx** file for that purpose.

We will also create a business layer class which will be used to get data from **Db using EF [Entity Framework]**.

There is going to be another class library project where we will keep our **Model / Entity** classes.

Here is the brief list of **steps** that we will go through in this chapter

1. Create Data Layer Class library project

1. Setup Database connection.
2. Create an Edmx file.
3. Update Db Model to add / update Db. Tables
4. Do T4 and build the project

2. Create a Database connection in server explorer in visual studio.

1. Create Db table/tables
2. Update Database

3. Create Model / Business Entity Class library project

1. Add your model or business entity classes
2. Reference this project where it needed.

4. Create a web Api Project or use the one created in Chapter 1

1. Add a new controller OR
2. Change/ Rename existing "Values Controller" to Employee Controller
3. Reference here Business Layer Library project
4. And start using its interface

5. Running the ASP.Net Web Api project see how it works.

1. Make sure that you have a web server running
2. Hosting web api on IIS OR IIS Express.
3. Build it and run.

Create Data Layer Class library project

Since we are going to work with **Entity Framework 6 (EF)**,

So, let's start with Setting up the database First. Why because we a following **Db First Approach** here

In the examples used in this book we will be using **SQL server Express** version.

So let's start.

Open **Server Explorer in Visual Studio**.

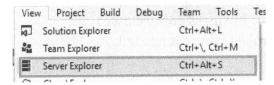

Then click on **server explorer** it will open and following things in it.

1. Azure connection
2. Database connection list
3. Server list

We will use the second one **"Database connection"**

Right click on **Database Connections** and then select

Add Connection…

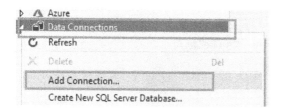

When you click on **add connection**

a window pane will open up where in you need to provide Data base details on your machine

if everything is provided correctly then

A new connection will be created which you can give name to it whatever you want, and, in this example, we have called it **"EmployeeEntities"**

Now we have a **Database connection,** lets add few **Db tables** and use them.

Here is how we can add **Database tables.**

Right click on **Data Connections** then on the connection which you created
Here it's called **"EmployeeEntities"**

expand it then list of **Db object** will come up
Right click on **"Tables"** then select
"Add New Table"

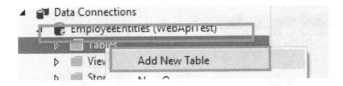

Once you click **"Add New Table"**

the following window pane will open.

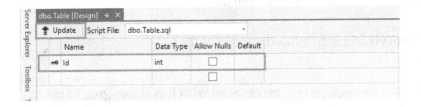

Here you can define the Database tables their columns and give a name.

Once you are done with table definition then you can click **"Update"** button

On click of this button your **Db table** will be created in Database.

Now you can start using Db table in EF project which you will create in next section.

In the examples which we have used

in this book we have created a database table

called **"Employee"**

And we will be using this table in our demonstration of how to add database tables using **Entity Framework's**

Database model or rather edmx file.

Since we are done with database creation. The reason we did that is we are following **Db First Approach**

Next thing we will do is start coding our data classes.

Since we are going to work with **Entity Framework 6 (EF)**,

So, let's start with setting up the database layer first.

And for that lets first add a class library project and give it a name. In the examples used in this book we called it

"EMPLOYEEDAO"

The reason why it's called such is that this is our Data Access Object holder library and it will hold Employee database table related stuff.

Naming projects with related functions helps.

Here is how you can create a Data Layer class library.

Go to solution explorer and right click on the solution there

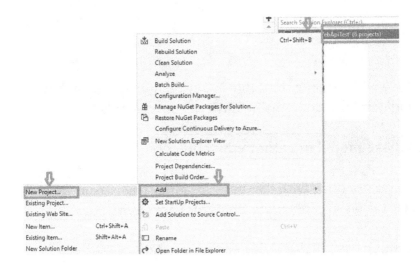

And then select add and then new project.

Click on new project then following window pane will appear.
Select **.NET standard project template** here and then select a **class library** project
Name it and say **OK**

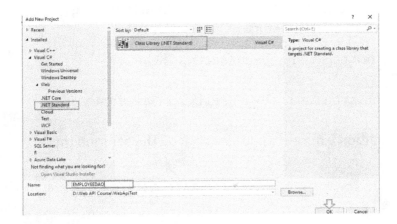

Once you have added a **class library project** then what you have to do is;

Add an **EDMX file** to this project and start creating our **Database model** set up.

Here is how you can do that.

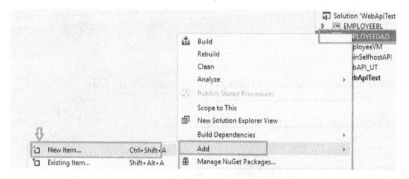

Right click on the data library project in solution explorer then select **"Add"**.

When you click on **"Add"** and then **"New Item"** the following window pane will open.

Here we need to select **"Data"** then **"ADO.NET Entity Data Model"**

Give it a name, in this example we called it

"EmployeeModel"

Now click **"Add"**

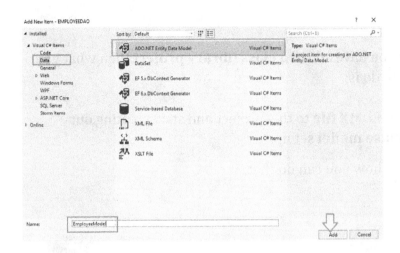

Once edmx file is added then we can open it in visual studio

Then right click on it and then select "Update Model from Database"

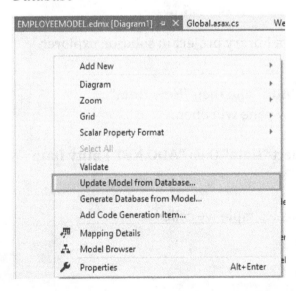

When you click on this option a windows dialog box will open where you can provide all data connectivity information and say next

Then you get options to;

1. **Add new Db table to the model**
2. **Update existing Db table in the model**
3. **Deleting existing Db table from the model**

since we are adding tables first time you can expand Add table **"Tab"**

Where you get list of all table and select the table which are required.

And the click Finish button as shown here.

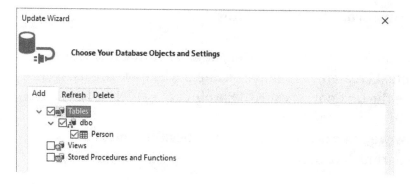

Once we are done with adding table to edmx Db model

You will see the list tables on the edmx model.

Now we have to do couple of things listed here.

1. Do T4 Template
2. Rebuild the solution

For T4 select Build menu in visual studio and then click on

"Transform All T4 Templates"

And then rebuild the solution, now we start using the Db context created, here in the example which we are using in here the Db Context called **"EmployeeEntities".**

Now we can use this EmployeeEntities Db context to get data from data base.

In the example which we are in this book we have created a business layer the code for that is given below.

This interface and class contains all the CRUD operations required for employee table.

```
public interface IEmployeeBL
    {
        IList<Employee> GetEMPLOYEEList();
        IList<Employee> GetEMPLOYEEBYId(int
Id);
        void UpdateEMPLOYEE(Employee
employee);
        void AddEMPLOYEE(Employee employee);
        void DeleteEMPLOYEE(int Id);
    }


public class EmployeeBL : IEmployeeBL
    {
        DbContext dbContext = new
EmployeeEntities();

        public void AddEMPLOYEE(Employee
employee)
        {
            using (var dbContext = new
EmployeeEntities())
            {
                EMPLOYEE empNew = new
EMPLOYEE();
                empNew.EmployeeName =
employee.EmployeeName;
                empNew.EmployeeId =
employee.EmployeeCode;
                empNew.Salary =
employee.Salary;
                dbContext.SaveChanges();
                var Employees =
```

```
dbContext.Set<EMPLOYEE>();
            Employees.Add(empNew);
            dbContext.SaveChanges();
        }
    }

    public void DeleteEMPLOYEE(int Id)
    {
        using (var dbContext = new
EmployeeEntities())
        {
            EMPLOYEE empDelete =
dbContext.EMPLOYEEs.Where(x => x.EmployeeId ==
Id).SingleOrDefault();

dbContext.EMPLOYEEs.Remove(empDelete);
            dbContext.SaveChanges();

        }
    }

    public IList<Employee>
GetEMPLOYEEBYId(int Id)
    {
        using (var dbContext = new
EmployeeEntities())
        {
            var query = (from Emp in
dbContext.EMPLOYEEs.Where(x=>x.EmployeeId ==
Id)
                        select new
Employee { EmployeeName = Emp.EmployeeName,
EmployeeCode = Emp.EmployeeId, Salary =
```

```
Emp.Salary, Category = Emp.Category });

                return query.ToList();
        }
    }



  public IList<Employee> GetEMPLOYEEList()
        {
            using (var dbContext = new
EmployeeEntities())
            {
                var query = (from Emp in
dbContext.EMPLOYEEs
                            select new
Employee { EmployeeName = Emp.EmployeeName,
EmployeeCode = Emp.EmployeeId, Salary =
Emp.Salary, Category = Emp.Category });

                return query.ToList();
        }
    }



public void UpdateEMPLOYEE(Employee employee)
        {
            using (var dbContext = new
EmployeeEntities())
            {
                EMPLOYEE empUpdate =
dbContext.EMPLOYEEs.Where(x => x.EmployeeId ==
employee.EmployeeCode).SingleOrDefault();
```

```
                empUpdate.EmployeeName =
employee.EmployeeName;
                empUpdate.EmployeeId =
employee.EmployeeCode;
                empUpdate.Salary =
employee.Salary;
                dbContext.SaveChanges();

            }
        }
    }
```

Now we have this BL[Business layer] class which we can use in api controllers for respective CRUD api operation / actions

Here is the api controller code which is used in the example in this book.

```
 public class EmployeeController :
ApiController
    {
        IEmployeeBL iEmployeeBL = new
EmployeeBL();

        public IList<Employee> Get(int Id)
        {
```

```
        return
iEmployeeBL.GetEMPLOYEEBYId(Id);
        }

        public IList<Employee>
GetEmployeeList()
        {
            return
iEmployeeBL.GetEMPLOYEEList();
        }

        public IList<Employee>
GetEmployeeListNew()
        {
            return
iEmployeeBL.GetEMPLOYEEList();
        }

        public void PostEmployee(int
EmployeeCode,string EmployeeName, string
Salary)
        {
            iEmployeeBL.AddEMPLOYEE(new
Employee { EmployeeCode= EmployeeCode,
EmployeeName = EmployeeName, Salary= Salary});
        }


public void Put ()
        {
            iEmployeeBL.UpdateEMPLOYEE(new
Employee { EmployeeCode = 1, EmployeeName =
"ABCXyz", Salary = "$2500" });
```

```
        }

        public void Delete(int id)
        {
            iEmployeeBL.DeleteEMPLOYEE(id);
        }
    }
```

So up to here we have setup

1. Database layer with entity framework
2. Coded BL
3. Have api controller methods for doing CRUD.

For testing api we can use a tool like postman or Rest API testing tool for chrome from google.

We can also create a web application and have the pages inside that app make api calls.

Now here in this book we have used post man to test all CRUD operation on api controllers.

Supporting OData query options in Asp.Net Web Api.

Here in this section we will see how we can use OData query Option in ASP.Net Web API,

What are OData Query options: There can be a requirement where in client sends some parameters in request URI and those parameters are applied on server side to perform the desired actions while getting data from api service interface.

Here are the various parameters that can be used together with api URI in request.

- $expand
- $filter
- $inlinecount
- $orderby
- $select
- $skip
- $top

Here are the examples of some the most used parameter with web API URI.

http://localhost/api/Employees?$expand=DeptId

http://localhost/api/Employees?$filter=Id ge 5 and Price le 15

http://localhost/api/Employees?$inlinecount=allpages

http://localhost/api/Employees?$orderby=Id desc

http://localhost/api/Employees?$select=EmployeeName, Salary

http://localhost/api/Employees?$skip=10

http://localhost/api/Employees?$top=5

Now to implement support for OData Query Options we have to do few things listed down here

-Install package 'Microsoft.AspNet.WebApi.OData.5.7.0'

-Enable support for OData query options in Web API Configuration class.

```
public static class WebApiConfig
{
    public static void
Register(HttpConfiguration config)
    {

        config.EnableQuerySupport();

        // Web API routes
        //config.MapHttpAttributeRoutes();

        config.Routes.MapHttpRoute(
            name: "DefaultApi",
            routeTemplate:
"Api/{controller}/{id}",
            defaults: new { id =
RouteParameter.Optional }
        );
    }
}
```

This setting will enable OData Query Support at global level.

But If we want to enable OData query support for only one controller method then we call apply [Queryable] attribute to the controller action.

```
[Queryable]
public IEnumerable<string> Get()
{
    return new string[] { "value1",
"value2" };
}
```

One that's done then we can start using query option in our API calls.

Limiting Query Options

With OData query options come with a feature called "limiting query option" with that we can put a limit on what type of query option can be used while calling a certain api action

Here are some the examples how we can use limitation on query options

```
[Queryable
(AllowedQueryOptions=AllowedQueryOptions.Top |
AllowedQueryOptions.Skip)]
```

- This will limit usage to only top and skip.

```
[Queryable (AllowedOrderByProperties="Id")]
```

- we can use comma separated property name like Id, EmployeeName etc.

```
[Queryable
(AllowedLogicalOperators=AllowedLogicalOperato
rs.Equal)]
```

- This will limit usage to only equal.

If we want to apply these limitations at global level,

then we can do that also.

By adding query attribute to the enable query support method in WebApiConfig.cs as shown below

```
        var queryAttribute = new
QueryableAttribute ()
            {
            AllowedQueryOptions =
AllowedQueryOptions.Skip |
AllowedQueryOptions.OrderBy,
                MaxTop = 40
            };
```

Query Validation

[Queryable] attribute performs query validation before executing it. It performs the validation by using the following method.

QueryableAttribute.ValidateQuery

We have the liberty of customizing this feature also. For that we need to write a custom class which need to inherit from **EnableQueryAttribute** class and write custom query attribute class which will be inherited from **OrderByQueryValidator** class. As shown below

```
public class MyQueryableAttribute:
EnableQueryAttribute
    {
        public override void
ValidateQuery(HttpRequestMessage request,
ODataQueryOptions queryOptions)
        {
            if (queryOptions.OrderBy != null)
            {
                queryOptions.OrderBy.Validator
= new MyOrderByValidator();
            }
            base.ValidateQuery(request,
queryOptions);
        }
    }

    public class MyOrderByValidator :
OrderByQueryValidator
    {
        public override void
Validate(OrderByQueryOption orderByOption,
ODataValidationSettings validationSettings)
        {
            if
(orderByOption.OrderByNodes.Any(node =>
```

```
node.Direction ==
OrderByDirection.Descending))
        {
            throw new ODataException("you
can not use 'desc' with this method call");
        }
        base.Validate(orderByOption,
validationSettings);
    }
  }
```

Once that is done do the build if there are errors, add the required references and nuget packages.

When the project is built, then we can **use [MyQueryable]** attribute on the controller method to use

the custom query validator. As shown below and you should be all set.

```
    [MyQueryable]
    public IQueryable<Employee>
GetAllEmployees(ODataQueryOptions opts)
        {
            if (opts.OrderBy != null)
            {
                opts.OrderBy.Validator = new
MyOrderByValidator();
            }
            var settings = new
ODataValidationSettings()
            {
            };
```

```
            var Employeelist =
iEmployeeBL.GetEMPLOYEEList();
            opts.Validate(settings);
            IQueryable results =
opts.ApplyTo(Employeelist.AsQueryable());
            return results as
IQueryable<Employee>;
        }
```

Chapter 2 Recap

So this chapter we discussed about

Creating a ASP.Net Web API
Then created a Data Layer project with Entity Framework

Created a BL class to get data from EF

then demonstrated how to create an api controller having CRUD.

Chapter 3

ASP. Net Web API and Routing Actions

In this chapter we will be covering the following things

1. Routing in ASP. Net Web API
2. Attribute Routing in ASP. Net Web API
3. Web Api And Exception Handling

So let's first start with Web API routing feature.

Web API Routing, how it works

ASP.NET Web API has api controller which is class and this class is responsible to all handle all HTTP requests coming to the api application.

Api controller contains actions methods, which do the work, API framework maps the Http requests to these methods.

Now how does API framework determine which action method it need to invoke, the Web API framework has got something called routing table. This is the place it maintains the mappings to api actions.

Well Asp.net web Api comes with features of defining routes to manage
controller action calls in web api.

To determine which method to call on controller api framework uses a Routing Table

When we create an Api project in visual studio by default api project template
defines api routes as shown below

```
config.Routes.MapHttpRoute(
    name: "DefaultApi",
    routeTemplate: "Api/{controller}/{id}",
    defaults: new { id = RouteParameter.Optional }
);
```

each entry in Routing table contains a route template.

When api framework
receives an http call it tries to match the calling Uri with the templates

if the match is not found then clients will get http 404 error

Why do we need routing?
Yes its very interesting question why routing?

Well there can be a requirement of managing api calls by

1. Categorizing and grouping them
2. Using certain keywords
3. using a certain pattern

So this feature helps a lot in the conditions where api have lots of endpoints.

Variation in asp.net web api routing.

In this section we are going to describe routing variations and how to achieve that.

For that we can use the features like

Http Verbs

Here are the http verbs that can be used with Asp.net web api

[HttpGet]
[HttpPut]
[HttpPost]
[HttpDelete]
[HttpHead]
[HttpOptions]
[HttpPatch]

In asp.net web api we can use multiple Http Verbs for a single actions

as shown below.

```
[AcceptVerbs("GET", "HEAD")]
public IList<Employee> GetEmployeeList()
{
    return iEmployeeBL.GetEMPLOYEEList();
}
```

Not only that we can use custom verb also

for example

```
// WebDev Method
[AcceptVerbs("MKCOL")]
public IList<Employee> GetEmployeeListNew()
{
    return iEmployeeBL.GetEMPLOYEEList();
}
```

Here one thing to note is this [Acceptverbs] attribute which takes care of what
verbs are available for an api action.

Routing by Action Names

Web api define one cool way of using Routing by action name also.

Here is an example using that style of routing

```
config.Routes.MapHttpRoute(
    name: "ActionApi",
    routeTemplate: "api/{controller}/{action}/{id}",
    defaults: new { id = RouteParameter.Optional }
);
```

Here if you see after controller the action name is used.

But for this method/way of routing we need to define [Http]

get or post or any

other attribute along with the action name on the methods

as shown below.

```
[HttpGet]
[ActionName("GetCustomImage")]
public IList<Employee> Get(int Id)
{
    return iEmployeeBL.GetEMPLOYEEBYId(Id);
}
```

Non-Actions

Asp.net web api also provide one features

called "Non Actions"

If we use this attribute then we can stop the calls to this
method.

```
[NonAction]
public IList<Employee> Get(int Id)
{
    return iEmployeeBL.GetEMPLOYEEBYId(Id);
}
```

Attribute Routing in Web API

As we discussed in earlier section

Routing is what is used to match a Uri to an action in web

api.

But Web api defines one more style of routing and that's

called Attribute Routing

In this type of routing web api uses attributes to define the routes

by this style of routing you can define routes, by which we can have better control

over how we can work with routes.

For example we can define a hierarchy of resources.

Now the question come why should we go for attribute routing?

The previous release of Web API used convention routing.

This type of routing defines one or more route templates, When Api framework receives a request, it matches the URI against the route template.

But there is an issue with convention-based routing, it makes it difficult to support certain Uri styles

for example
http://api/salesrep/1/orders

now these types of Uri definitions are very simply to create with the help of

Attribute Routing

```
[Route("salesrep/{salesrepId}/orders")]
public IList<Employee> Get(int Id)
{
    return iEmployeeBL.GetEMPLOYEEBYId(Id);
}
```

Usage of Attribute Routing

Here are the usage of attribute routing

1. Api Versioning.

With the help of attribute routing we can do versioning in web api action methods.

Here is an example of the same.

```
[Route("employee/V1/Category")]
public IList<Employee> GetEmployeeList()
{
    return iEmployeeBL.GetEMPLOYEEList();
}
[Route("employee/V2/Category")]
public IList<Employee> GetEmployeeListNew()
{
    return iEmployeeBL.GetEMPLOYEEList();
}
```

Here we have implemented two versions of an api action method. Which can be used with different hosts to get the data.

Also, for one client application we can provide version V1 and for another we can provide version V2 for same api action method.

Next usage of Attribute Routing is
Having Overload Uri segments.

Something like this

```
[Route("employee/department/1")]
public IList<Employee> GetEmployeeList()
{
    return iEmployeeBL.GetEMPLOYEEList();
}
[Route("employee/department/NewJoinees")]
public IList<Employee> GetEmployeeListNew()
{
    return iEmployeeBL.GetEMPLOYEEList();
}
```

Another usage of attribute routing is

having multiple parameter types

like EmployeeId, dob as shown here.

```
[Route("employee/department/1")]
public IList<Employee> GetEmployeeList(int Id)
{
    return iEmployeeBL.GetEMPLOYEEList();
}
[Route("employee/department/dob")]
public IList<Employee> GetEmployeeListNew(DateTime dob)
{
    return iEmployeeBL.GetEMPLOYEEList();
}
```

Enabling Attribute Routing

Now let's see how we can enable attribute routing in asp.net web pi

we need to do the following things

1. Add setting in WebApiConfig.cs class
2. Use [Route] attribute on controller action

Here are the setting required in web api configuration class.

```
//Web API routes
config.MapHttpAttributeRoutes();

config.Routes.MapHttpRoute(
    name: "DefaultApi",
    routeTemplate: "Api/{controller}/{id}",
    defaults: new { id = RouteParameter.Optional }
);
```

And then start using [Route] attribute on controller actions.

As shown here.

```
[Route("employee/department/1")]
public IList<Employee> GetEmployeeList(int Id)
{
    return iEmployeeBL.GetEMPLOYEEList();
}
```

Web Api and Exception/Error Handling

Asp.net web api framework offers couple of ways of

dealing with exceptions and errors

Here are these ways/styles

1. HttpResponseException
2. ExceptionFilters
3. HttpError

Lets first work with **HttpResponseException**

When a https call is make to api and something breaks

then either it's the internal server error
or it's the whole exception stack what client gets.

Now with the help of HttpResponseException class we can

return a desired response code to the clients, here is an
example of how we can use HttpResponseException class.

```
[Route("employee/department/1")]
public IList<Employee> GetEmployeeList(int Id)
{
    IList<Employee> empList = iEmployeeBL.GetEMPLOYEEList();
    if (empList == null)
    {
        var resp = new HttpResponseMessage(HttpStatusCode.NotFound)
        {
            Content = new StringContent(string.Format("No Employee with Id = {0}", Id)),
            ReasonPhrase = "Employee Id Not Found"
        };
        throw new HttpResponseException(resp);
    }
    return empList;
}
```

In this example shown above, when an http request comes in

the employee list is pulled from database,

but if this does not return any data then a more precise message is returned to

the caller

Woking with ExceptionFilters

We have the liberty of customizing the way Web API handles exceptions with the help of writing an exception filter.

 An exception filter is executed when a controller method throws an unhandled exception which is not an HttpResponseException error

Exception filters implement the System.Web.Http.Filters.IExceptionFilter interface.

Here is the simplest way of implementing an exception filter. For that we need to
write a custom exception filter class

 which is derived from the System.Web.Http.Filters.ExceptionFilterAttribute class

and override the OnException method.

```
public class NotImplExceptionFilterAttribute : ExceptionFilterAttribute
{
    public override void OnException(HttpActionExecutedContext context)
    {
        if (context.Exception is NotImplementedException)
        {
            context.Response = new HttpResponseMessage(HttpStatusCode.NotImplemented);
        }
    }
}
```

After creating this class implementation, we need to register it in

Web Api configuration class.

As shown here.

```
// Web API configuration and services
config.Filters.Add(new NotImplExceptionFilterAttribute());

config.Routes.MapHttpRoute(
    name: "DefaultApi",
    routeTemplate: "Api/{controller}/{id}",
    defaults: new { id = RouteParameter.Optional }
);
```

Now the exception filter is applied in the api

at global level, any call which results in errors on api side will

invoke this filter and a response will be given to the caller.

Woking with HttpError Class

The HttpError class defines a consistent way to handle and respond with error information in the response body.

Here is an example which shows how we can return HTTP status code 404

by using HttpError in the api response

```csharp
public HttpResponseMessage GetEmployee(int id)
{
    IList<Employee> empList = iEmployeeBL.GetEMPLOYEEList();
    if (empList == null)
    {
        var message = string.Format("Employee with id = {0} not found", id);
        return Request.CreateErrorResponse(HttpStatusCode.NotFound, message);
    }
    else
    {
        return Request.CreateResponse(HttpStatusCode.OK, empList);
    }
}
```

CreateErrorResponse method

which is defined in the
System.Net.Http.HttpRequestMessageExtensions class.

CreateErrorResponse creates an HttpError instance

and then creates an HttpResponseMessage

which contains the HttpError.

One advantage of using HttpError is it goes through the content negotiation

and serialization process like any strongly typed model.

And response in this case will be either XML or Json based of media type selected in api.

Chapter - 3 Recap

So this chapter we discussed about

Creating Routing variations with Web api

Also worked with attribute routing

And in the end worked HttpResponseException, Exception Filters and

HttpError for gracefully handling errors in web api

Chapter - 4

ASP. Net Web API Data Formats

In this chapter we will learn to support additional

media types formats in asp.net web api.

What are media types?

Media types also called MIME types and are responsible for defining

how a piece of data is formatted.

Examples of Internet media types

text/html
image/png
application/json

so from these examples we can see that every media type contains two parts

a type and a subtype.
In web api a media type determines how
web api serializes or deserializes the http message body.

Asp.net web api has in built support for
xml, json, bson and urlencoded data

and additionally it can support some custom media types also like

csv, pdf etc.

And that can be achieved by creating a custom Media Formatter.

For that it provides two classes called

1. MediaTypeFormatter. This class uses asynchronous read and write methods.

2. BufferedMediaTypeFormatter. This class is derived from MediaTypeFormatter but uses synchronous read/write methods.

In the following example we are going show

how we can serialize an employee class object into

a comma-separated-values (CSV) format

Now to start with let's see what is needed to do that.

1. We need to create custom formatter class which will be derived from

BufferedMediaTypeFormatter

Here is the code that.

```
public class ProductCsvFormatter :
BufferedMediaTypeFormatter
    {
        public ProductCsvFormatter()
        {
            SupportedMediaTypes.Add(new
MediaTypeHeaderValue("text/csv"));
            SupportedEncodings.Add(new
UTF8Encoding(encoderShouldEmitUTF8Identifier:
false));

SupportedEncodings.Add(Encoding.GetEncoding("i
so-8859-1"));
        }
        public ProductCsvFormatter(
MediaTypeMapping mediaTypeMapping) : this()
        {

MediaTypeMappings.Add(mediaTypeMapping);
        }

        public
ProductCsvFormatter(IEnumerable<MediaTypeMappi
ng> mediaTypeMappings) : this()
        {
            foreach (var mediaTypeMapping in
mediaTypeMappings)
            {

MediaTypeMappings.Add(mediaTypeMapping);
            }
```

```
        }

        public override bool CanReadType(Type
type)
        {
            return false;
        }



        public override bool
CanWriteType(System.Type type)
        {
            if (type == typeof(Product))
            {
                return true;
            }
            else
            {
                Type enumerableType =
typeof(IEnumerable<Product>);
                return
enumerableType.IsAssignableFrom(type);
            }
        }


        private string WriteItem(Product
product, StreamWriter writer)
        {
            return writer.ToString();
        }
```

```csharp
public override void WriteToStream(Type type,
object value, Stream writeStream, HttpContent
content)
        {
            Encoding effectiveEncoding =
SelectCharacterEncoding(content.Headers);

            using (var writer = new
StreamWriter(writeStream))
            {
                var product = value as
IEnumerable<Product>;
                if (product != null)
                {
                    foreach (var prod in
product)
                    {
                        string prodCsv =
WriteItem(prod, writer);
                    }
                }
                else
                {
                    var singleProduct = value
as Product;
                    if (singleProduct == null)
                    {
                        throw new
InvalidOperationException("Cannot serialize
type");
                    }
                    string prodCsv =
```

```
WriteItem(singleProduct, writer);
            }
        }
    }



    static char[] _specialChars = new
char[] { ',', '\n', '\r', '"' };

        private string Escape(object o)
        {
            if (o == null)
            {
                return "";
            }
            string field = o.ToString();
            if
(field.IndexOfAny(_specialChars) != -1)
            {
                return
String.Format("\"{0}\"", field.Replace("\"",
"\"\""));
            }
            else return field;
        }
    }
```

compile the code by doing build.

Now next step is to register this class in web api
configuration class.

registering custom media type class in web api configuration class.

Here is how we do that.

```
config.Formatters.Clear();
config.Formatters.Add(new BsonMediaTypeFormatter());
config.Formatters.Add(new ProductCsvFormatter());
```

Once you are done with these settings now you can call your

controller action and you find that api is now returning a

CSV file and its getting downloaded.

Now let have a look at how can enable json and Xml serialization.

Xml and Json both media types formatter are provided by

Asp.Net web api by default no extra setting is required

to enable these two formatters,

But we need to
understand that at a time only one type of
formatter can work either xml or json.

Apart from that there are some choices that can be made while using these formatters.

Like

By default, JsonMediaTypeFormatter uses the Json.NET library to do object serialization.

This Json.NET is a third-party library which is open source though.

So you have a choice of not using it.

now instead of this you can use DataContractJsonSerializer

for we need to do the following settings in config class of web api

```
var json = GlobalConfiguration.Configuration.Formatters.JsonFormatter;
json.UseDataContractJsonSerializer = true;
```

same is true with xml formatter too.
Which we will see in next section.

XmlMediaTypeFormatter uses the DataContractSerializer by default for doing serialization.

Again here we can decide whether we want to use

XmlMediaTypeFormatter to work with XmlSerializer or DataContractSerializer.

If we want to use XmlSerializer the we need to set
UseXmlSerializer property to true

as shown here.

```
var xml = GlobalConfiguration.Configuration.Formatters.XmlFormatter;
xml.UseXmlSerializer = true;
```

Now next things which we will look at is

How to remove formatters

In asp.net web api we have choice of removing the JSON
formatter

or the XML formatter from the list of formatters.

Here are the reasons why we might have to do that

1. We Want to restrict our web API calls to a particular
media type response only.
like we may decide to support only JSON and not XML
formatter.

2. The another reason could be we want to replace default
formatter with a custom formatter.
like having csv formatter

Here is the code which removes the default formatters.

We need to place this Application Start method, in Global.asax.

```
// Remove the JSON formatter
config.Formatters.Remove(config.Formatters.JsonFormatter);

// Remove the XML formatter
config.Formatters.Remove(config.Formatters.XmlFormatter);

// Remove both formatters
config.Formatters.Clear();
```

Bson Support in Asp.Net Web Api

What is Bson?

Bson stands for binary json, but BSON and JSON are serialized very differently.

Why we use Bson?

Here are some of the points which could be the reason behind
having bson formatter in your api

1. While working with image bson is good fit because the bson payload gets smaller than json payload in this case.

2. encoding and decoding of Bson payload is much faster, reason being numeric values are stored as number rather than strings

But one thing here to note is

bson format is good for the scenarios where your clients are other than web browsers only.

How to enable Bson support in web api.

Just apply these settings in asp.net web api configuration class.

```
public static class WebApiConfig
{
    public static void Register(HttpConfiguration config)
    {
        config.Formatters.Add(new BsonMediaTypeFormatter());
    }
}
```

Once this setting is done, then your api calls

will start returning bson data.

Chapter - 4 Recap

So this chapter we discussed about

Working with media type formatters in web api

created a custom csv media formatter and used it.

Then we also looked at how to use json and xml formatters differently

and in the end we worked with Bson formatter

Chapter - 5

ASP. Net API Testing and debugging

In this chapter we will see how to do Unit Testing for web api controller. Since Unit testing is one of the basic needs of a software so it can be great if we can do unit testing of web api code.

There is a mechanism of unit testing api code, which we will learn here.

Here are the things we will discuss in detail, and these are the steps which we will follow in this chapter.

1. How to include a Unit Test Project in your solution and
2. Write simple Unit test and
3. How to debug a unit test and run it.

Let's start with creating a unit test project in your solution using visual studio.

open solution explorer and right click on the solution.

Then select add as shown below.

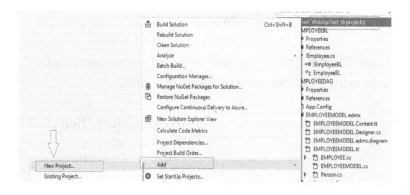

When you click on new project then

A new dialog box will open,

In this dialogue box select "Test" in the left pane and then select "Unit Test Project" template in right pane.

And then say OK

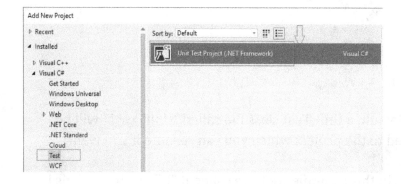

Before you click OK in this windows pane

Make sure to give a proper name to your test project, that's the name which will be used for your test project.

After you have given a proper name to the project, then click Ok

Once you do that visual studio will create test project and will add in your solution. Which you can see in solution explorer as shown below.

That should look something like this

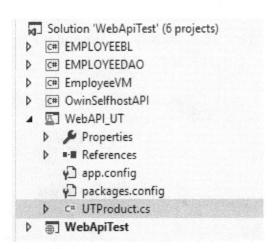

By default, a Unit Test class file called "UnitTest1" will be added to the project which you can rename if you want.

Here in this example we have called it "UTProducts" This is the unit test class where we will be using for our unit tests or rather test methods.

Now let's create test methods in this class.

Here is the code where a simple unit test method is created.

```
[TestClass]
public class UTProduct
{
    [TestMethod]
    public void GetProducts()
    {
        // Arrange
        var controller = new ProductsController();
        controller.Request = new HttpRequestMessage();
        controller.Configuration = new System.Web.Http.HttpConfiguration();

        // Act
        var response = controller.Get();

        // Assert
        Assert.AreEqual(1, response.productid);
        Assert.AreEqual("Product1", response.productname);
    }
}
```

Here in this test method we are initializing an api controller

then request object is created required configuration is done

and then the controller method "Get" is called

after that we are checking the result returned by

controller method.

You can see here there are two assert calls

one checking product Id and another one checking its name.

These assert calls can be used to do any kind of checking in the response.

This will vary based on the return type of the

controller methods.

Now we will see two things here

1. Debug the test
2. And run it.

Let's debug the unit test. For that we have to open unit test class and go to

the Test Method which we want to debug

then right click and say Debug test

something like this.

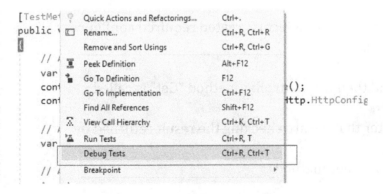

When you click on Debug test, visual studio will start compilation and do the build once build is done then it will start running unit test in debug mode,

And if a break point is placed then we can see the execution control

coming into test method code as shown below.

```
13        public void GetProducts()
14        {
15            // Arrange
16            var controller = new ProductsController();    ≤ 1ms elapsed
17            controller.Request = new HttpRequestMessage();
18            controller.Configuration = new System.Web.Http.HttpCon
19
20            // Act
21            var response = controller.Get();
22
23            // Assert
24            Assert.AreEqual(1, response.productid);
25            Assert.AreEqual("Product1", response.productname);
```

You can execute it step by step by pressing F10 and see the response

and assert results.

Now let's Run the unit test. For that we have to open unit test class and go to

the Test Method which we want to run

then right click and say run test

something like this.

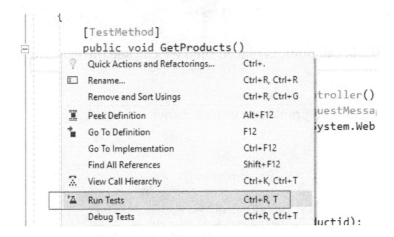

When you click on Run test, visual studio will start compilation and do the build

once build is done then it start running unit test,

And if a break point is placed then the execution control will not

stop in this case, it will ignore break point and simply run and finish execution

then the results will be shown in Test Explorer winnow as shown here

Testing Web Api Service

For testing Asp.Net Web Api we can use the following methods.

1. Create Custom http client in a console app
2. Create a web application and call service from web pages
3. Use RestApi testing tool from Google
4. Or use some other tool like postman.

In the example we will be using postman you can download postman and start using it. It's quite simple and have more features.
So here we are using it

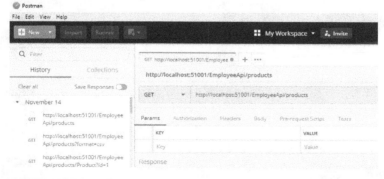

Here we can provide the action Uri of web api service and click on "send" button, once we click on send button postman will send a request to api application by calling your api URL

Now if you want to debug code of your web api, then make sure that the api application is running in debug mode in visual studio and you have "Debug Break Points" at the right place [where ever you want to debug the code]

Chapter - 5 Recap

So this chapter we learned about

How we can do unit testing in Asp.Net Web Api

Chapter - 6

ASP. Net API Deployment and Hosting

In this chapter we will see

How to host a web api service in owin, IIS and IIS Express.

Let's start with Owin

in order to host our api with owin we need to follow these steps

1. Create a console application
2. Install owin package by nuget package in this project
3. Configure Web Api for Self-Host
4. Doing coding for owin host
5. Then testing the host environment

To create console app open solution explorer and

right click on the solution and then add - > new project

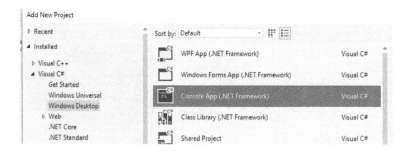

Then from this window select project templates select console app give a name to it

and say ok.

 The console application will be created

Now we need to install the owin support
for that run the following command on nuget

command window.

Install-Package Microsoft.AspNet.WebApi.OwinSelfHost

This will install the required package for owin.

Now we need to add a StartUp class to this project

This class will have the configuration settings in it.

Let's add this class.

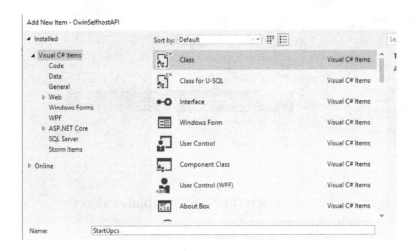

Then copy the below code to it.

```csharp
namespace OwinSelfhostAPI.Properties
{
    using Owin;
    using System.Web.Http;

    namespace OwinSelfhostSample
    {
        public class Startup
        {
            public void
Configuration(IAppBuilder appBuilder)
            {
                HttpConfiguration config = new
HttpConfiguration();
                config.Routes.MapHttpRoute(
                    name: "DefaultApi",
                    routeTemplate:
"api/{controller}/{id}",
```

```
                    defaults: new { id =
RouteParameter.Optional }
                );
                appBuilder.UseWebApi(config);
            }
        }
    }
}
```

Now we need to add a Web Api Controller.

Let's do that then copy the below code to it.

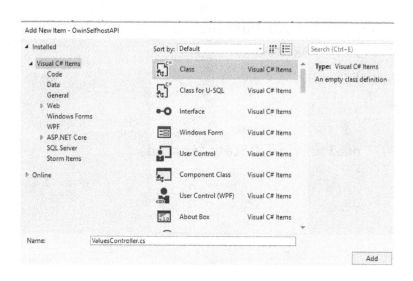

```
public class ValuesController : ApiController
    {
        public IEnumerable<string> Get()
        {
```

```
            return new string[] { "value1",
"value2" };
        }

        public string Get(int id)
        {
            return "value";
        }

        public void Post([FromBody]string
value)
        {

        }

        public void Put(int id,
[FromBody]string value)
        {

        }

        public void Delete(int id)
        {

        }
    }
```

Now we need to go to program class do the following things there.
1. Define BaseUri for service host
2. And start the host using this base uri
3. Create an httpClient and call the controller action in the

service uri
4. Get the response from the call and write it to console.

Here is the code for the program class.

```
namespace OwinSelfhostAPI
{
    class Program
    {

        static void Main(string[] args)
        {
            string baseUri =
"http://localhost:8080";
            Console.WriteLine("Starting web
Server...");
            WebApp.Start<Startup>(baseUri);

            // Create HttpCient and make a
request to api/values
            HttpClient client = new
HttpClient();
            var response =
client.GetAsync(baseUri +
"/api/Values").Result;

            Console.WriteLine(response);

Console.WriteLine(response.Content.ReadAsStrin
gAsync().Result);
            Console.WriteLine("Server running
at {0} - press Enter to quit. ", baseUri);
            Console.ReadLine();
```

```
        }
    }
}
```

Once that's done then run the console app and see what happens.

If everything goes good then you should see a window something like this

```
  D:\Web API Course\WebApiTest\OwinSelfhostAPI\bin\Debug\OwinSelfhostAPI.exe
Starting web Server...
StatusCode: 200, ReasonPhrase: 'OK', Version: 1.1, Content: System.Net.Http.Stre
{
  Date: Wed, 28 Nov 2018 15:34:57 GMT
  Server: Microsoft-HTTPAPI/2.0
  Content-Length: 19
  Content-Type: application/json; charset=utf-8
}
["value1","value2"]
Server running at http://localhost:8080 - press Enter to quit.
```

Now here we can see that api is hosted on the same uri which we defined, and its working, the call which we send to it worked properly.

Hosting Web API in Cloud

For hosting a web api in azure or on cloud we need to do the following things

1. First, we need to create a Microsoft azure project

2. Then Add the Owin package

3. Then Add an Http endpoint

To create azure project select cloud in installed templates and then

select Azure Cloud Service project. And then click OK

Now we need to add a worker role.

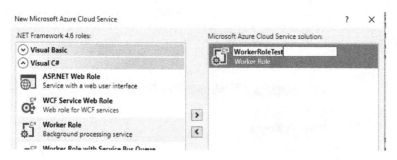

Once the project is created then we can install owin package.

To install Owin package just run the following command

on nuget command prompt

Install-Package Microsoft.AspNet.WebApi.OwinSelfHost

Now we need to add an Http Endpoint

for that go to worker role in solution explorer and right click on it

then select properties

On click of properties following window pane will open.

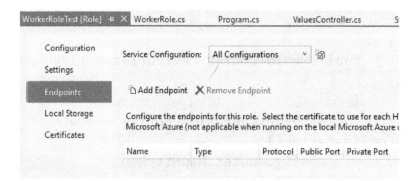

Now we need to add an end point here.

The following endpoint would be added to the worker role.

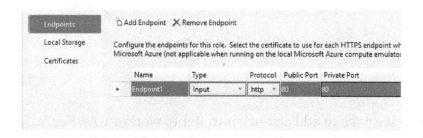

Now we need to configure web api self-host. For that

Right click on worker role
and add a new class called StartUp.cs

```
using Owin;
using System.Web.Http;
```

```
namespace WorkerRoleTest
{
    class Startup
    {
        public void Configuration(IAppBuilder
app)
        {
            HttpConfiguration config = new
HttpConfiguration();
            config.Routes.MapHttpRoute(
                "Default",
                "{controller}/{id}",
                new { id =
RouteParameter.Optional });

            app.UseWebApi(config);
        }
    }
}
```

Now we need to add an api controller to worker role. For that right click on worker role and select add new item and add a class and copy the following code to it.

```
public class MyController : ApiController
    {
        public HttpResponseMessage Get()
        {
            return new HttpResponseMessage()
            {
```

```
                Content = new
StringContent("Hello this is hoted in owin")
            };
        }



        public HttpResponseMessage Get(int id)
        {
            string message =
String.Format("Hello this is hoted in owin,
and is:", id);
            return new HttpResponseMessage()
            {
                Content = new
StringContent(msg)
            };
        }
    }
}
```

Now open the worker role class and copy this
code to it.

```
 public class WorkerRoleTest : RoleEntryPoint
    {
        private IDisposable _appAzure = null;

        public override void Run()
        {
            Trace.TraceInformation("Entry
point being called", "Info");
```

```
        while (true)
        {
            Thread.Sleep(5000);

Trace.TraceInformation("Starting", "Info");
        }
    }

    public override bool OnStart()
    {

ServicePointManager.DefaultConnectionLimit =
12;

        var myendpoint =
RoleEnvironment.CurrentRoleInstance.InstanceEn
dpoints["Endpoint1"];
        string baseUri =
String.Format("{0}://{1}",
            myendpoint.Protocol,
myendpoint.IPEndpoint);


Trace.TraceInformation(String.Format("Starting
OWIN at {0}", baseUri),
            "Information");

        _appAzure =
WebApp.Start<Startup>(new StartOptions(url:
baseUri));
        return base.OnStart();
    }
```

```
public override void OnStop()
{
    if (_appAzure != null)
    {
        _appAzure.Dispose();
    }
    base.OnStop();
}
}
```

We can run the app locally and test it, but if want it to be deployed on azure, then we have to publish and host it on azure and start using it.

Hosting Web api in IIS and IIS Express is very simple.

Let's start with IIS express

When we create a web api project in visual studio, by default all the
project are hosted on IIS express, or you call it development server

So actually your web api is by default hosted in IIS express. You can see that by going to api

project's properties window as shown here.

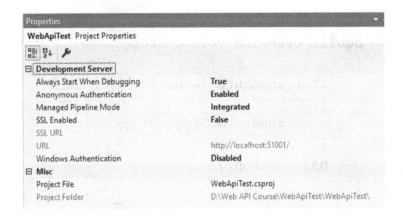

Now to host a web Api in IIS
you can do the followings

1. Install IIS on your machine
2. Open IIS management console
3. Then create a virtual directory in IIS
4. And point it the physical directory where api project is placed
and make it application, that's it your api is hosted in IIS.

Chapter - 6 Recap

So this chapter we learned about

How we can Self host a Web Api application using Owin

How to Host an Asp.Net Web Api in in cloud with Azure

And finally, how to host it in IIS and IIS Express.

Chapter - 7

Advance Topics

Section will see **How we can enable https in ASP.Net Web Api.** We will start with discussing all the steps required to enable https in asp.net web api. And then we will discuss all the steps in details. Also, you will see how we can enable https support for development server.

Enabling https in ASP.Net Web Api

Steps to enable https in ASP.Net web Api.

- Write a custom class which is inherited from **AuthorizationFilterAttribute** class.
- Register that class in ASP.Net Web Api Config
- Apply [RequireHttps] attribute on Api controller actions.
- Create a temporary certificate for SSL.
- Install the certificate
- Enable Https support to development server in visual studio.

Write a custom class which is inherited from AuthorizationFilterAttribute

Write a custom class as shown below.

```
public class RequireHttpsAttribute:
AuthorizationFilterAttribute

    {
```

```
        public override void OnAuthorization
(HttpActionContext actionContext)
        {
        if
(actionContext.Request.RequestUri.Scheme ! =
Uri.UriSchemeHttps)
        {
                actionContext.Response = new
HttpResponseMessage
(System.Net.HttpStatusCode.Forbidden)
                {
                    ReasonPhrase = "HTTPS
Required for this call"
                };
        }
        else
        {

base.OnAuthorization(actionContext);
        }
    }
}
```

Register that class in ASP.Net Web Api Config

To register custom http filter class in web api configuration here are the settings.

// Web API configuration and services

config.Filters.Add(new RequireHttpsAttribute());

Remember this a global setting and will require all controller methods to run on https.

If we want to have few methods to run on http then in that case, just disable this setting. And use the [Requirehttps] attribute for individual methods.

Apply [RequireHttps] attribute on Api controller actions.

```
[RequireHttps]
public IEnumerable<string> Get ()
{
        return new string [] { "value1",
"value2" };
}
```

Note: We need to use this [RequireHttps] attributes only in case we need to enable https only for selective api controller actions. Otherwise Web Api configuration global settings are enough.

But if are targeting only few api methods to run on https then we must disable the global configuration. Other wise all methods calls will demand https.

Create a temporary certificate for SSL.

To create a temp certificate run the following command in command prompt.

makecert.exe -n "CN=Development CA" -r -sv TempCA.pvk TempCA.cer

It will ask for password when you will run this command on your machine.

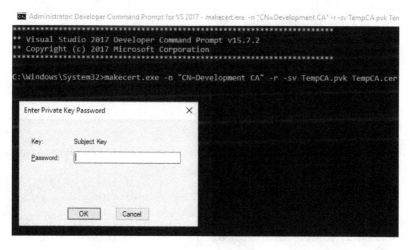

once the certificate is created it will be saved on your machine at the path selected in command prompt windows. As shown here.

```
Administrator: Developer Command Prompt for VS 2017
**********************************************************
** Visual Studio 2017 Developer Command Prompt v15.7.2
** Copyright (c) 2017 Microsoft Corporation
**********************************************************

C:\Windows\System32>makecert.exe -n "CN=Development CA" -r -sv TempCA.pvk TempCA.cer
Succeeded

C:\Windows\System32>_
```

Now we need to install it.

Install the certificate

For installing the certificate on your local machine, you need to do the following steps.

- Open MMC (Management console) window
- Then go to File - > Add or Remove Snap Ins

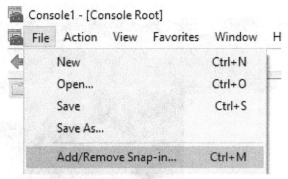

- Then select Certificates from available Snap Ins
- Then click on ADD button
- Then select Computer account in the window pane that opens
- Then select Local Computer Account
- Then click next and OK

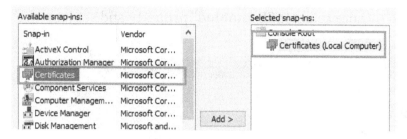

Now the certificate snap in added to MMC.

Now we need to install the certificated by selecting it in snap in

For that

- Go to Certificates expand it.
- Then Select "Trusted root certification Authorities"
- Then Select Action - > All Tasks - > Imports
- Select the certificate and finish.

Now temporary certificate is installed on your computer.

This certificate will be used for SSL communication on your machine, but apart from installation you need to do anything with respect to certificates.

Now next step is to enable Https for development server.

Enable Https support to development server in visual studio

For that do the followings

- open your web api solution in visual studio,
- Then select the web api project in solution explorer.
- Select **View** Menu in visual studio
- Now select "Properties window" or click F4.
- A window pane will open.

- There select **"SSL Enabled"** property and set it to **true**

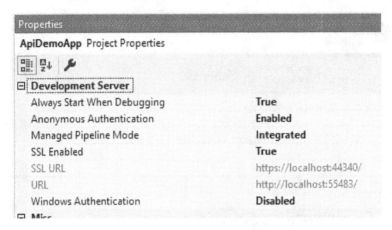

Now the development server is ready to work with https too.

Dependency Injection in Asp.Net Web Api.

What is dependency injection: A dependency is an object is required by another object to function properly.

Here we are going to show what is the benefit of dependency injection and how we can use it with asp.net web api.

Here is an example where we are having an api controller class with a dependency called

```
11    public class ValuesController : ApiController
12    {
13
14        private IProductRepository productRepository = new ProductRepository();
15
16        [Route("api/values/V1/Category")]
17        public IList<Product> Get()
18        {
19            return productRepository.GetAllProducts();
20
21        }
```

Now the code a line number 14 is ok it will work but we can avoid it.

Why because it is initializing a repository class which can happen at some common location and be separated from here.

This where Dependency comes into the picture.

With the help of dependency Injection, we can handle initialization of all the dependent object for class.

In this example we are going to use constructor injection, mean the depend object are passed on via constructors.

Now have look at the example below.

```
public class ValuesController : ApiController
{
    private IProductRepository _repository;

    public ValuesController(IProductRepository productRepository)
    {
        _repository = productRepository;
    }
    public ValuesController()
    {
    }
    [Route("api/values/V1/Category")]
    public IList<Product> Get()
    {
        return _repository.GetAllProducts();
    }
```

Here ProductResository class object is being passed from the constructor.

Here the problem is we do not control api controller constructors. So, we cannot pass this object ourselves.

We need something which can take care of it. For that we will be using Microsoft Unit Framework.

Let's see in detail how to implement dependency injection in web api, here are the steps.

1. Install-Package Unity
2. Create a Dependency resolver class
3. Implement interface "IDependencyResolver" in Dependency resolver class
4. Register Dependency resolver class in Api Config
5. And the define two constructors in Api Controller one with parameter and another without parameter
6. Then define a private variable of the Dependency [ProdcutRespository]class inside controller class
7. And use that for repo calls

Let's start with Unit package installation.

Run the following command on nuget command prompt.

Install-Package Unity

This will install the unity framework in your project.

Now here is the code for dependency resolver class.

```
using System;

using System.Collections.Generic;

using System.Linq;

using System.Web;

using System.Web.Http.Dependencies;

using Unity;

using Unity.Exceptions;


namespace ApiDemoApp
{
    public class DependencyResolver :
IDependencyResolver
    {
        protected IUnityContainer container;
        public
DependencyResolver(IUnityContainer container)
        {
            this.container = container;
        }


        public object GetService(Type
serviceType)
        {
```

```
            try
            {
                return
container.Resolve(serviceType);
            }
            catch (ResolutionFailedException)
            {
                return null;
            }
        }


    public IEnumerable<object>
GetServices(Type serviceType)
        {
            try
            {
                return
container.ResolveAll(serviceType);
            }
            catch (ResolutionFailedException)
            {
                return new List<object>();
            }
```

```
        }


        public IDependencyScope BeginScope()
        {
            var child =
container.CreateChildContainer();
            return new
DependencyResolver(child);
        }


        public void Dispose()
        {
            Dispose(true);
        }


        protected virtual void Dispose(bool
disposing)
        {
            container.Dispose();
        }
    }
}
```

Now we need to register this dependency class in api configuration class.

This how we do that.

```
// Web API configuration and services
var container = new UnityContainer();
container.RegisterType<IProductRepository, ProductRepository>(new HierarchicalLifetimeManager());
config.DependencyResolver = new DependencyResolver(container);

// Web API routes
config.MapHttpAttributeRoutes();
```

This is that place where we tell the unity container which classes to initialize once this setup is done then we are good to use the controller code without explicitly initializing the repo class.

Now let's have look at the api controller code.

```
public class ValuesController : ApiController
{
    private IProductRepository _repository;

    public ValuesController(IProductRepository productRepository)
    {
        _repository = productRepository;
    }
    public ValuesController()
    {
    }
    [Route("api/values/V1/Category")]
    public IList<Product> Get()
    {
        return _repository.GetAllProducts();
    }
}
```

Here we can see that the repo class is object is passed to the controller's constructor and the initialization of repo class is done by Unity.

Here is repo class code

using System;

```csharp
using System.Collections.Generic;

using System.Linq;

using System.Text;

using System.Threading.Tasks;

namespace ProductRepo.Products
{
    public interface IProductRepository
    {
        IList<Product> GetAllProducts();
    }


    public class ProductRepository :
IProductRepository
    {
        public IList<Product> GetAllProducts()
        {
            return new List<Product>() { new
Product {ProductId = "01", ProductName =
"iPhone", ProductPrice = "Inr 50k" } };
        }
    }
}
```

So, this how we can use dependency injection in Asp.net web api.

Using Mocking for Entity Framework with Asp.Net web api

Here are the steps required to implement mocking for unit testing web api code.

1. Create a test project
2. Create an Api controller
3. Add dependency injection
4. Add EF nuget to test project
5. Create a test Db context in test project
6. Create a TestProduct DbSet
7. Then create a test context
8. Now create a Unit Test class and test methods

We can add a test project to the existing which we are using in this book as an example. If not, then create a new api application and add a new test project.

Once that's done, then what we can do is add a new controller to the the api project as shown below.

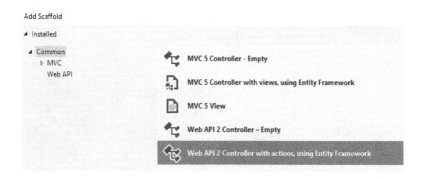

Here is controller code

```
using System;
using System.Collections.Generic;
using System.Data;
using System.Data.Entity;
using System.Data.Entity.Infrastructure;
using System.Linq;
using System.Net;
using System.Net.Http;
using System.Web.Http;
using System.Web.Http.Description;
using ApiDemoApp.Models;
using ProductRepo.Products;

namespace ApiDemoApp.Controllers
{
    public class TestProductsController :
ApiController
    {
        private ApiDemoAppContext db = new
ApiDemoAppContext();

        public IQueryable<Product>
GetTestProducts()
```

```
        {
            return db.Products;
        }

        [ResponseType(typeof(Product))]
        public IHttpActionResult
GetTestProduct(string id)
        {
            Product product =
db.Products.Find(id);
            if (product == null)
            {
                return NotFound();
            }

            return Ok(product);
        }

        [ResponseType(typeof(void))]
        public IHttpActionResult
PutGetTestProduct(string id, Product product)
        {
            if (!ModelState.IsValid)
            {
                return BadRequest(ModelState);
            }

            if (id != product.ProductId)
            {
                return BadRequest();
            }

            db.Entry(product).State =
EntityState.Modified;

            try
```

```
        {
            db.SaveChanges();
        }
        catch
(DbUpdateConcurrencyException)
        {
            if (!TestProductExists(id))
            {
                return NotFound();
            }
            else
            {
                throw;
            }
        }

        return
StatusCode(HttpStatusCode.NoContent);
    }

    [ResponseType(typeof(Product))]
    public IHttpActionResult
PostGetTestProduct(Product product)
    {
        if (!ModelState.IsValid)
        {
            return BadRequest(ModelState);
        }

        db.Products.Add(product);

        try
        {
            db.SaveChanges();
        }
        catch (DbUpdateException)
```

```
        {
            if
(TestProductExists(product.ProductId))
            {
                return Conflict();
            }
            else
            {
                throw;
            }
        }

        return
CreatedAtRoute("DefaultApi", new { id =
product.ProductId }, product);
        }

        [ResponseType(typeof(Product))]
        public IHttpActionResult
DeleteGetTestProduct(string id)
        {
        Product product =
db.Products.Find(id);
            if (product == null)
            {
                return NotFound();
            }

            db.Products.Remove(product);
            db.SaveChanges();

            return Ok(product);
        }

        protected override void Dispose(bool
disposing)
```

```
        {
            if (disposing)
            {
                db.Dispose();
            }
            base.Dispose(disposing);
        }

        private bool TestProductExists(string
id)
        {
            return db.Products.Count(e =>
e.ProductId == id) > 0;
        }
    }
}
```

Now we have to have dependency injection in place, here is the code for that.

```
using ProductRepo.Products;
using System;
using System.Collections.Generic;
using System.Data.Entity;
using System.Linq;
using System.Web;
namespace ApiDemoApp.Models
{
    public interface IApiDemoAppContext :
IDisposable
    {
        DbSet<Product> Products { get; }
        int SaveChanges();
        void MarkAsModified(Product product);
    }
```

```
    public class ApiDemoAppContext :
DbContext, IApiDemoAppContext
    {
        public ApiDemoAppContext() :
base("name=ApiDemoAppContext")
        {
        }
        public DbSet<Product> Products { get;
set; }
        public void MarkAsModified(Product
product)
        {
            Entry(product).State =
EntityState.Modified;
        }
    }
}
```

Now let's go to the test project and add entity framework reference via nuget.

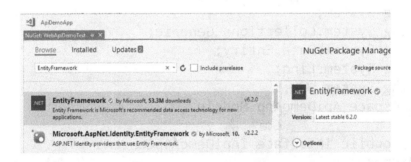

And the also we need to install Microsoft.AspNet.WebApi.Core to the test project, that too we can do by using nuget manager.

Once that's done then We need to create a Test context in test project.

```
using System;
using System.Collections.Generic;
using System.Collections.ObjectModel;
using System.Data.Entity;
using System.Linq;

namespace ApiDemoApp.Tests
{
    public class TestDbSet<T> : DbSet<T>,
IQueryable, IEnumerable<T>
        where T : class
    {
        ObservableCollection<T>
_dataTestCollection;
        IQueryable _dataTestQuery;

        public TestDbSet()
        {
            _dataTestCollection = new
ObservableCollection<T>();
            _dataTestQuery =
_dataTestCollection.AsQueryable();
        }

        public override T Add(T item)
        {
            _dataTestCollection.Add(item);
            return item;
        }

        public override T Remove(T item)
        {
            _dataTestCollection.Remove(item);
```

```csharp
            return item;
        }

        public override T Attach(T item)
        {
            _dataTestCollection.Add(item);
            return item;
        }

        public override T Create()
        {
            return
Activator.CreateInstance<T>();
        }

        public override TDerivedEntity
Create<TDerivedEntity>()
        {
            return
Activator.CreateInstance<TDerivedEntity>();
        }

        public override
ObservableCollection<T> Local
        {
            get { return new
ObservableCollection<T>(_dataTestCollection);
}
        }

        Type IQueryable.ElementType
        {
            get { return
_dataTestQuery.ElementType; }
        }
```

```
        System.Linq.Expressions.Expression
IQueryable.Expression
        {
            get { return
_dataTestQuery.Expression; }
        }

        IQueryProvider IQueryable.Provider
        {
            get { return
_dataTestQuery.Provider; }
        }

        System.Collections.IEnumerator
System.Collections.IEnumerable.GetEnumerator()
        {
            return
_dataTestCollection.GetEnumerator();
        }

        IEnumerator<T>
IEnumerable<T>.GetEnumerator()
        {
            return
_dataTestCollection.GetEnumerator();
        }
    }
}
```

No we need to a Test DbSet here is the code for it.

```
using ApiDemoApp.Tests;
using ProductRepo.Products;
using System;
using System.Collections.Generic;
using System.Linq;
```

```
using System.Text;
using System.Threading.Tasks;

namespace ApiDemoApp.Tests
{
    class TestProductDbSet :
TestDbSet<Product>
    {
        public override Product Find(params
object[] keyValues)
        {
            return
this.SingleOrDefault(product =>
product.ProductId == (int)keyValues.Single());
        }
    }
}
```

Now need to add a Repository context. Here is the code for it.

```
using ApiDemoApp.Models;
using ApiDemoApp.Tests;
using ProductRepo.Products;
using System;
using System.Collections.Generic;
using System.Data.Entity;
using System.Linq;
using System.Text;
using System.Threading.Tasks;

namespace WebApiDemoTest.Tests
{
    public class TestProductRepoContext :
IApiDemoAppContext
```

```
        {
            public TestProductRepoContext()
            {
                this.Products = new
TestProductDbSet();
            }

            public DbSet<Product> Products { get;
set; }

            public int SaveChanges()
            {
                return 0;
            }

            public void MarkAsModified(Product
item) { }
            public void Dispose() { }
        }
}
```

Now we need to create unit test. Here the code.

```
using System;
using ApiDemoApp.Controllers;
using ApiDemoApp.Models;
using
Microsoft.VisualStudio.TestTools.UnitTesting;
using ProductRepo.Products;

namespace WebApiDemoTest
{
    [TestClass]
    public class Test_ProductController
```

```
{
    [TestMethod]
    public void GetProduct_ById()
    {
        var contextTest = new
ApiDemoAppContext();

        var controllerTest = new
TestProductController(contextTest);
        var result =
controllerTest.GetProduct(3);

        Assert.IsNotNull(result);
        Assert.AreEqual(3,
result.Content.Id);
    }
}
}
```

This is how we can do Unit testing for ASP.Net web API.

Chapter - 7 Recap

So, in this chapter we learned about

How to enable https in Asp.Net web api,

How to do entity framework mocking for unit testing Web API code

How to use dependency injection in Asp.Net Web api

Chapter - 8
Validation in Web API

Validation is can be very important part of Web API implementation in scenarios where data is critical. Although some people may argue on whether web api request validation be done always or in specific scenarios only. Well it does not matter what kind of Web API is being developed, we should make it a practice of validating web api request before we process it.

Web API Request Validation Techniques

There two approached which we discussed here

1. Data Annotations
2. IValidatableObject Interface

Using Data Annotations for Validation

We can use Data Annotations in ASP.NET Web API for validation of model, what you can do is use attributes from the `System.ComponentModel.DataAnnotations` namespace which help in setting validation rules on properties of your model.

Here is an example of using Data Annotations on Models:

```
using System.ComponentModel.DataAnnotations;
namespace ApiDemoApp.Models
{
    public class MyProduct
    {
        public int ProductId {get; set; }
        [Required]
        public string ProductName { get; set; }
        public decimal Price { get; set; }
        [Range(0, 999)]
        public double Weight { get; set; }
    }
}
```

You may be familiar with model validation in ASP.NET MVC, its almost the same thing here. We need to use an attribute called "Required" This attribute will make sure that the property where this attribute is used must not be null. Similarly Range attribute means that Weight must be between zero and 999.

Now let's assume that we get the Json form of the above mentioned MyProduct model which looks something like this.

JSON Data {"ProductId ":100, "Price":11.99, "Weight":50}

Here we can see that the client application is not including the ProductName property, which is marked as required in the model definition.

So, what happens is Web API converts the JSON into a MyProduct instance, that is when the validations are fired on MyProduct model for corresponding validation attributes.

We can do the validation of model in our controller class only as shown below.

```
using ApiDemoApp.Models;

using System.Net;

using System.Net.Http;

using System.Web.Http;


namespace ApiDemoApp.Controllers
{
    public class MyProductController :
ApiController
    {
        public HttpResponseMessage Post (MyProduct
myProduct)
        {
            if (ModelState.IsValid)
            {
                // Here you do the processing
needed by client.
```

```
                return new
HttpResponseMessage(HttpStatusCode.OK);

        }

        else

        {

        // If Model state is invalid then we
respond back with the following response.
                return
Request.CreateErrorResponse(HttpStatusCode.BadReque
st, ModelState);

        }

    }

  }

}
```

With Data annotations-based Model validation we cannot be sure that data coming from client is safe or not. The Web API developer may have to perform some sort of other validation in other part of the web API application.

One simple example to handle this case can be to enforce key constraints at Database level.

There is something called "Under-Posting" in web API Under-posting happens when the client does not send out all the properties skipping few.

Using IValidatableObject Interface for Validations

```
using System;
using System.Collections.Generic;
using System.ComponentModel.DataAnnotations;

namespace ProductRepo.Products
{
    public class Product : IValidatableObject
    {
        public int ProductId { get; set; }
        public string ProductName { get; set; }
        public decimal ProductPrice { get; set; }

        public IEnumerable<ValidationResult>
Validate(ValidationContext validationContext)
        {
            if (Math.Abs(ProductPrice) < 0)
            {
                yield return new
ValidationResult("Invalid Product Price");
            }
        }
    }
}
```

Then we have to create an action filter class which will implement OnActionExecuting method of ActionFilterAttribute interface.

The example of action filter class is shown below.

```
using System.Net;

using System.Net.Http;

using System.Web.Http.Controllers;

using System.Web.Http.Filters;


namespace ApiDemoApp.Filters
{
    public class ValidationModelStateFilter :
ActionFilterAttribute
    {
        public override void
OnActionExecuting(HttpActionContext actionContext)
        {
            if (!actionContext.ModelState.IsValid)
            {
                actionContext.Response =
actionContext.Request.CreateErrorResponse(HttpStatu
sCode.BadRequest, actionContext.ModelState);
            }
        }
    }
}
```

After than we need to add this class to the web api configuration as shown below.

```
using System.Web.Http;
namespace ApiDemoApp
{
    public static class WebApiConfig
    {
        public static void
Register(HttpConfiguration config)
        {
            // Web API configuration and services
            config.Filters.Add(new
ValidationModelStateFilter());


            config.Routes.MapHttpRoute(
                name: "DefaultApi",
                routeTemplate:
"api/{controller}/{id}",
                defaults: new {id =
RouteParameter.Optional }
            );
        }
    }
}
```

Then we can run the api and the methods call and the results.

Chapter - 8 Recap

So, in this chapter we learned about

How to use Data Annotations for model validation in Asp.Net web api,

How to Use IValidateObject Interface in Web API code

Chapter - 9

Authentication and Authorization in web API

Authentication and Authorization in ASP.NET Web API

After we finish creating web, we may want to have control over who can access it. in this chapter we understand to pull access control in asp.net web api.

We are going to discuss both authentication and authorization in this chapter.

What is authentication?

Authentication is the process of making sure that the user is the one who he or she claims to be.

Suppose there is user called John, when he logs into the web api we can use authentication mechanism be sure of that John is actual John.

That can be done verifying the user and one more information called password, which is normally kwon by John only.

What is Authorization?

In same way Authorization is the process of deciding what actions a user can perform while running/using the app.

The example of authorization is a User may not have access to admin features like resetting user password in the web api.

The Web API technology is designed in such a way that it assumes that authentication will be done at the host. If your web api is using web-host, then the host is IIS, and as we know that IIS uses HTTP modules for authentication purpose.

We have the liberty of configuring web api application to use any of the authentication types which are provided by IIS or provided by ASP.NET.

And if you do not want to use IIS and ASP.Net based authentication then you are free to write your own HTTP module to perform custom authentication for your web api application.

Here little more on how authentication works in IIS.

When a request comes for web api endpoint it creates an object of principal class which basically is an IPrincipal object and it represents the security context under which code is running.

Now what happens next is this principal object is tied to the Thread which is doing the execution. That can be done using Thread.CurrentPrincipal.

There is an Identity object in the principal object which basically contains user level information. The host uses this information for authenticating the user.

If the authentication module in the host finds that the user is authentications correctly

Then it sets Identity.IsAuthenticated property returns true.

If the web api is being called by anonymous user in that case IsAuthenticated will return false.

Setting the Principal while using custom authentication.

If your application using any custom authentication logic, in that case you must set the principal at the following two places

Thread.CurrentPrincipal.

This property is the standard way to set the thread's principal in .NET

HttpContext.Current.User.

This property is specific to ASP.NET.

The following code shows how to set the principal:

```
private void SetPrincipal(IPrincipal
principal)
{
    Thread.CurrentPrincipal = principal;
    if (HttpContext.Current != null)
    {
        HttpContext.Current.User = principal;
    }
}
```

If you are using a web host, you must set the principal in both places.

Otherwise the security context will become inconsistent.

If you are suing self-hosting in that case HttpContext.Current is null. We should check for null before assigning to HttpContext.Current as shown Above.

How to use Authorization in Web API

The process of Authorization happens little later in the http pipeline and happens closer to the api controller.

Which helps the developer to write more granular code which can be used for when you grant access to any Web api resource.

Web host Authorization filters run just before the controller action are executed. In case the request is not authorized, the Authorization filter returns an error response, and the action method is not called.

While the execution is within a controller action, we have full control over the current principal from the ApiController.User property.

Which you can use to filter a list of resources based on the user name. And returning only the resources which belong to that user.

How to use [Authorize] Attribute

There is a built-in authorization filter which is used along with Authorize Attribute on a controller class. This built-in filter verifies whether the user is authenticated. If not, then it returns HTTP status code 401 which means Unauthorized user request, and it will stop the web api action invocation.

This attribute-based filters can be applied globally or at the controller level or at the level of individual actions methods.

Applying filter Globally use the following settings in web api configuration class.

As shown below.

```
public static void Register(HttpConfiguration
config)
{
    config.Filters.Add(new AuthorizeAttribute());
}
```

Applying filter at Controller level, as shown below.

This can be used to restrict access for specific Controller, here is how attribute can be added to the Controller

```
[Authorize]
public class ValuesController : ApiController
{
    public HttpResponseMessage Get(int id) {  }
    public HttpResponseMessage Post() {  }
}
```

Applying filter at Action level

This can be used to restrict access for specific actions, here is how attribute can be added to the action method

```
public class ValuesController : ApiController
{
    public HttpResponseMessage Get() {  }

    [Authorize]
    public HttpResponseMessage Post() { }
}
```

Alternatively, you can restrict the controller and then allow anonymous access to specific actions, by using the [AllowAnonymous] attribute.

In the following example, the Post method is restricted, but the Get method allows anonymous access.

```
[Authorize]
public class ValuesController : ApiController
{
    [AllowAnonymous]
    public HttpResponseMessage Get() {  }

    public HttpResponseMessage Post() {  }
}
```

In the examples which we just talked about, the authorization filter allows any authenticated user to access the restricted methods and only anonymous users are restricted.

Now also have the luxury of limiting access to specific users or to users in specific roles

Here is how that can be done.

```
// Restriction by specific users
[Authorize(Users="John,Bob")]
public class ValuesController : ApiController
{

}
```

```
// Restriction by specific role:
[Authorize(Roles="Administrators")]
public class ValuesController : ApiController
{

}
```

The AuthorizeAttribute filter class for Web API controllers is in the System.Web.Http namespace.

Writing Custom Authorization Filters for web api

To write a custom authorization filter, you need to drive your class from one of these types

AuthorizeAttribute.

You need to extend this class to perform authorization logic based on the current user and the user's roles.

AuthorizationFilterAttribute.

You will need to extend this class to perform synchronous authorization logic that is not necessarily based on the current user or role.

IAuthorizationFilter.

You will need to Implement this interface to perform asynchronous authorization logic.

Using Authorization Inside a Controller Action

In some cases, you might allow a request to proceed, but change the behaviour based on the principal. In such case you can put a check for the user role and do the desired action.

Here is how It can be used.

```
public HttpResponseMessage Get()
{
    if (User.IsInRole("Administrators"))
    {

    }
}
```

Chapter - 9 Recap

So, in this chapter we learned about

How to use Authentication for securing Asp.Net web api,

How to Use Authorizations in Web API code

Chapter - 10

Caching in web API

Unfortunately caching in asp.net web api is not available out of box. Like we have caching in asp.net web api is missing that part.

But there are ways which can help in having caching work in asp.net web api.

In asp.net web api we can use MemoryCache object to use caching feature.

This class is part of **System.Runtime.Caching** namespace

To use this class, we can add a reference to the assembly where this name space is located.

Right click on the web api project and then select add reference. And the search for **System.Runtime.Caching** in assembly list. Then add this assembly reference as shown below

Reference Manager - ApiDemoApp

▲ Assemblies

Framework		Name	Version
Extensions	☑	System.Runtime.Caching	4.0.0.0
Recent		System.Runtime.DurableInstancing	4.0.0.0
Search Results		System.Runtime.InteropServices.RuntimeInfor...	4.0.1.0
		System.Runtime.Remoting	4.0.0.0
▷ Projects	☑	System.Runtime.Serialization	4.0.0.0
		System.Runtime.Serialization.Formatters.Soap	4.0.0.0
▷ COM			
▷ Browse			

Once the reference is added you can use MemoryCache class for cache management in web API.

Here is an example of how you can cache objects or data in a web api controller.

```csharp
using ProductRepo.Products;

using System;

using System.Collections.Generic;

using System.Linq;

using System.Runtime.Caching;

using System.Web.Http;


namespace ApiDemoApp.Controllers
{
    public class ValuesController : ApiController
    {
        public IQueryable<MyProduct> GetPersonalDetailsCached(bool isCached)
        {
            var cache = MemoryCache.Default;


            if (cache.Get("MyProduct") == null)
            {
                var cachePolicty = new CacheItemPolicy();
```

```
cachePolicty.AbsoluteExpiration =
DateTime.Now.AddSeconds(60);

                var data = db.MyProducts;

                cache.Add("MyProduct",
data.ToList(), cachePolicty);

                return data;
        }
        else
        {

                IEnumerable<MyProduct> data =
(IEnumerable<MyProduct>)cache.Get("MyProduct")
;

                return data.AsQueryable();
        }
    }
    }
}
```

Chapter - 10 Recap

So, in this chapter we learned about

How to use caching features in Asp.Net web api, by using MemoryCache object

----

Learning Evaluation

In this section we have decided to give project work to the readers/student.

The project Work.

1. Create a Web Api Application
2. In that try to implement all the features which are discussed in this book.
3. Mail that code to me I will go through it and will revert back
with feedback

My email is : lalitkumartalan@gmail.com

Note : This project work will help you gain full command over web api development if you do it honestly.

About the author

Lalit has about 17 years of Information Technology experience.

He started his career 2001 as software engineer.

Most of his experience is in Microsoft Technologies.

He holds a bachelor's degree in Mathematics and a post graduate computer diploma.

Has got certifications like MCP, MCAD, MCSD.Net, Scrum Developer and

Software Architect & Project Management from IIM Bangalore.

Quiz 1 Answers

1 - A

2 - A

3 - B

4 - B

5 - C

6 - B

7 - A

8 - B

9 - A

10 -E

Feedback

Your feedback is very important for me to improve this book.

Please share your thoughts about this book. No matter whether it's positive or otherwise. Just send a mail to me at the following email id.

Email: **lalitkumartalan@gmail.com**

www.ingramcontent.com/pod-product-compliance
Lightning Source LLC
Chambersburg PA
CBHW071249050326
40690CB00011B/2322